FRONTIERS OF AVIATION

David Jefferis

Illustrated by
Terry Hadler, Ron Jobson and
Michael Roffe

Franklin Watts
London   New York   Toronto   Sydney

First published in 1988 by
Franklin Watts
12a Golden Square
London W1R 4BA

First published in the USA
by Franklin Watts Inc.
387 Park Avenue South
New York, N.Y. 10016

First published in Australia
by Franklin Watts
Australia
14 Mars Road
Lane Cove, NSW 2066

UK ISBN: 0 86313 734 2
US ISBN: 0-531-10637-3
Library of Congress
Catalog Card No: 88-50378

Technical consultant
T Callaway, RAF Museum,
Hendon, London

Designed and produced by
Sunrise Books

© 1988 Franklin Watts

Printed in Belgium

FRONTIERS OF AVIATION

Contents

Introduction	4
Flightpath of advance	5
Through the sound barrier	6
Highest and fastest	8
Bigger and bigger	10
The incredible Harrier	12
Computers in control	14
Return of the propeller	16
Weird wings	18
Fighters of tomorrow	20
Airport 2000	22
After Concorde	24
Final frontiers	26
Air data	28
Record breakers	30
Glossary	31
Index	32

Introduction

Aviation has come a long way since the Wright Brothers' first flight of 1903. With Orville Wright as pilot, the *Flyer* covered a ground distance of 36.57 m (120 ft) or so, about half the fuselage length of a present-day Boeing 747 jet airliner.

In the 59 seconds of Orville's flight the 747 can fly nearly 16.5 km (10 miles), though the airliner is only a medium-speed aircraft – the Lockheed SR-71 flies at 3,220 km/h (2,000 mph), more than three times the 747's 960 km/h (600 mph) cruising speed.

Speed and size are not the only advances in aviation technology however. Just as important are reliability, safety and economy.

In this book you will read how aviation has advanced in recent years and see what aircraft of the near future will look like.

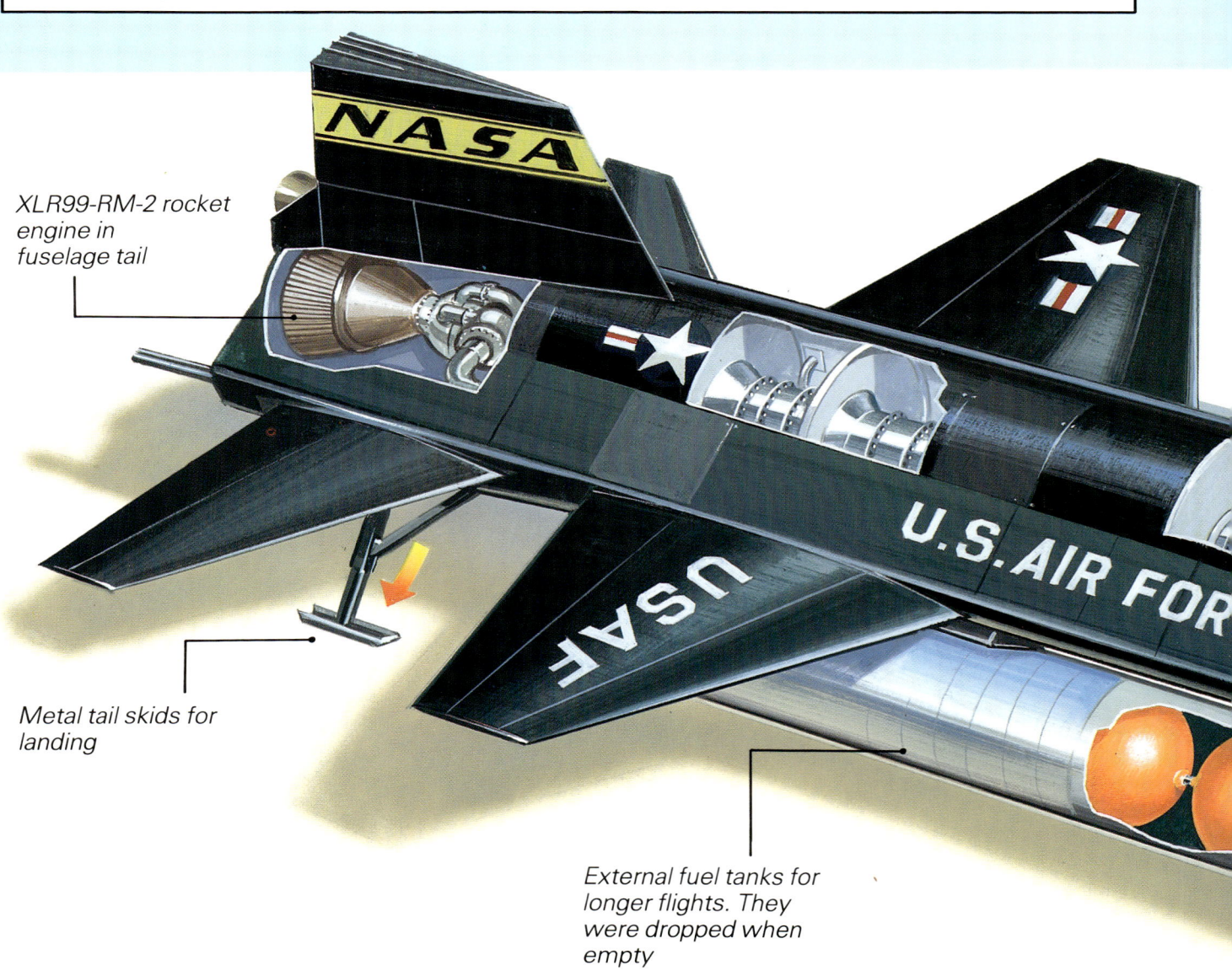

XLR99-RM-2 rocket engine in fuselage tail

Metal tail skids for landing

External fuel tanks for longer flights. They were dropped when empty

Flightpath of advance

The North American X-15 rocket plane blazed a high-speed trail through the skies in the 1960s. Information gained on research flights made in the plane led to the development of many of today's high speed machines, including the NASA Space Shuttle.

The long and slim X-15 included many design features found on today's high-speed craft, such as heat-resistant paint, rocket power and extremely thin wings.

Three X-15s were built, making 199 flights among them. Test pilot William Knight flew the last mission, on October 3, 1967. After 141.4 seconds of rocket burn, the X-15 reached the fantastic speed of 7,274 km/h (4,520 mph), a world record which still stands as the fastest winged flight ever.

Two X-15s had black paint. The third had a heat-resistant spray-on white coating

Cockpit fitted with an ejection seat for emergency escapes

On several missions X-15s flew higher than 80 km (50 miles), a height thought of as the "edge of space" Pilots on these high flights were awarded astronauts' wings

Normal controls were useless at high altitudes as the air was too thin to allow ailerons and rudder any "bite". X-15s had small "puffer jets" to give directional control

Pilot wore a shiny astronaut suit

Twin nose wheels

Through the sound barrier

Modern aviation really began after World War II. In the last years of the war the first jet-powered aircraft were developed in Germany, Britain and the United States.

Jets were much faster than propeller planes of the time but the big problem of high-speed flight turned out to be an invisible "wall" in the sky. Aircraft approaching Mach 1 – the speed of sound, 1,226 km/h (762 mph) at sea level – were buffeted by severe shock waves, and several pilots were killed as their planes were literally shaken to pieces in mid-flight. The dreaded "sound barrier" was widely regarded as impassable.

In fact, after much careful research and design, the sound barrier proved to be no barrier at all. The Bell X-1 rocket plane was specially built with very thin wings and a high-set tail to avoid shock wave problems.

Around 8.00 am on October 14, 1947, a B-29 Superfortress bomber trundled down the runway at Muroc Lake, California. Instead of bombs, the B-29 carried the X-1, painted bright orange and named *Glamorous Glennis*. Test pilot on the flight was Captain Charles "Chuck" Yeager, who had named the X-1 after his wife.

With a mighty roar from its four engines, the B-29 hurtled down the runway into the clear desert sky. At

The speed of sound

The speed of sound varies according to height and temperature. It travels fastest through the warm, dense air at sea level and slows down in the thin air of the stratosphere. Mach 1, 1,226 km/h (761 mph) at sea level, drops to a constant speed of about 1,062 km/h (660 mph) at height.

Bell X-1

Bell X-1A

△ Yeager's first supersonic flight was made in the bright orange aircraft he named after his wife Glennis. The X-1A was faster and had a raised cockpit canopy.

3,658 m (12,000 ft) Yeager climbed down a metal ladder through the bomb bay into the X-1's tiny cockpit. He had to use a piece of broomstick to lock the hatch as he had broken a rib the day before while horseriding and couldn't reach over far enough.

At 6,096 m (20,000 ft) Bob Cardenas, the B-29 pilot, eased the big plane into a shallow dive and with a "Let's get it over with" from Yeager over the radio, the X-1 dropped free of its shackles – and nearly into disaster. The dive speed was too slow and for several seconds Yeager had to fight the controls. Once he had the X-1 pointing smoothly down, he lit the rocket motor to thrust the plane into the deep blue sky.

At 12,802 m (42,000 ft) Yeager was flying at Mach .96. The ride got smoother the faster he flew, until suddenly the air speed indicator needle wobbled, then jerked right over. The X-1 had gone supersonic!

The sound barrier had been broken, with less fuss than anyone had dreamed possible. For 20 seconds Yeager kept the speed needle hard off the scale, before raising the X-1's nose a little to slow down. Then he dumped the remaining fuel. As planned, Yeager glided the craft down to land on Muroc's dried-out lake-bed runway.

The supersonic flight – later checked as Mach 1.015 – was kept a top secret for several months, but once word leaked out Yeager and the X-1 went into the history books.

Highest and fastest

The Bell X-1 was the first of many X-planes, all built as experimental aircraft to explore the frontiers of aviation. Speed was not the only research area. The X-5 of 1951, for example, had swing-wings, a design feature later built into the F-111 fighter-bomber. The 1958 X-14 was a small vertical takeoff jet with an open cockpit and fixed undercarriage.

The fastest and highest-flying X-plane of all was the North American X-15. This bullet-shaped rocket plane flew so fast it came up against the heat barrier. Heat is created by friction with air, in much the same way that your hands get hot if you rub them together. Temperatures in the nose of the X-15 reached 750°C or more – far greater than the hottest kitchen oven. An experimental solution to the heat problem was a spray-on mixture of resin and glass powder. This was designed as an ablative coating – it would burn away during flight, but another coat could be applied later.

On October 3, 1967, the gleaming white X-15A-2 fell away from the wing of its mother plane with Major William Knight at the controls. Knight fired the rocket motor and headed skywards. 67.4 seconds after ignition the external fuel tanks fell away, all their fuel exhausted. The X-15 carried Knight higher and faster. As the heat built up, the leading edges of the plane glowed cherry-red – then warning lights blinked on in the cockpit...

▷ X-15s were carried under the starboard wing of a giant B-52 Stratofortress bomber. During the 199 test flights many height and speed records were taken. An X-15 still holds the fastest powered flight by a winged aircraft. Orbital space vehicles are faster, though. Shuttle Orbiters glide down from space at speeds of over Mach 20.

Under the X-15's tail was a dummy ramjet, a new type of high speed engine, and the friction heat was burning through its support pylon. Then more warning lights blinked on, showing that the inside of the rear fuselage was heating up. Knight tried to dump the rest of his fuel, but the dump valves were wrecked. He brought the plane down as a glider, heavy with more than a tonne of explosive rocket fuel still aboard. Luckily the undercarriage held out as he eased the craft onto its lake-bed runway.

After the flight it was discovered that the ramjet had fallen into a nearby Air Force bombing range. The X-15's ablative coating was so badly charred and pitted that the plane was considered a write-off.

Despite this alarming flight, the three-plane X-15 programme was considered a major success. The rocket planes were flown by a dozen top test pilots, including Neil Armstrong, the first man on the Moon.

△ At the end of their missions, X-15s came in for glider landings.

Normally, any unused rocket fuel was dumped at height.

Bigger and bigger

Douglas DC-3

De Havilland Comet

Lockheed Hercules

Sleek-looking aircraft like the X-planes make the headlines, but airliners and cargo planes carry out the daily routine of moving vast numbers of people and quantities of material from place to place.

The Douglas DC-3 of 1935 was the first efficient airliner. Until then, no aircraft carried enough to make money for its operators. In the 1950s, jetliners such as the De Havilland Comet and Boeing 707 revolutionized airline flying. For the first time, passengers had a fast and quiet ride in the smooth air of the stratosphere. The first flight of the Boeing 747 in 1969 marked another revolution, the "jumbo jet" age of mass passenger travel.

Aircraft will get even bigger in the future. A French company, Hydro 2000, has plans for a 1000-tonne seaplane able to carry a 300-tonne cargo load. If passengers were carried, this could mean over 4,000 people on a single seaplane. Hydro 2000 claims its machine is suitable for those Third World countries which have no large airports or runways.

A popular present-day airlifter is the Lockheed Hercules, in service with many air forces and likely to be flying well into the 21st century. Only a medium-sized aircraft, the "Herky bird" has carried a jumbo-sized load on at least one occasion. On May 28, 1975, 452 Vietnamese refugees packed aboard a Herk. There was standing room only in the cavernous cargo bay. The plane became so crowded that 32 people crammed into the flight deck! Although the aircraft was at least 10 tonnes overweight – a normal load would be around 160 people – the pilot managed a takeoff after using all the runway. And he flew the refugees to safety, making a smooth landing at journey's end.

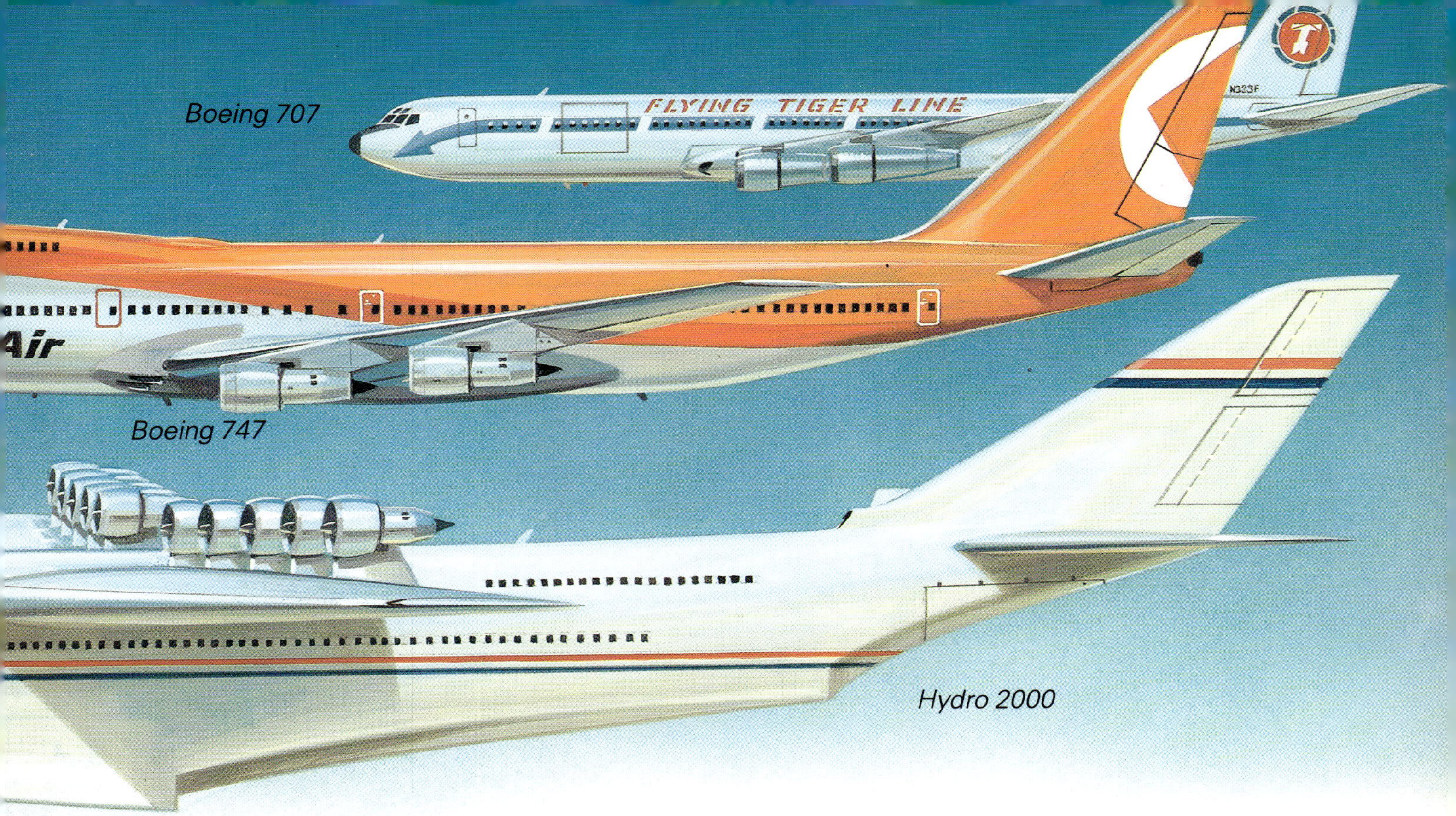

Boeing 707

Boeing 747

Hydro 2000

△ *Hydro 2000 compared with other transport aircraft. The 747 is currently the largest passenger-carrying jetliner. The giant seaplane would dwarf Boeing's jumbo-jet. Hydro 2000's design includes a lift-up nose section, for easy loading and unloading.*

▷ *An idea from the Lockheed aircraft company for a giant airlifter of the early 21st century. Most of the cargo is carried inside the deep main wing. Four jet engines are mounted behind the cockpit.*

The incredible Harrier

The Harrier is an aircraft that needs no runway. Its single jet engine has four nozzles which swivel down for takeoff. Jet exhaust thrusts the plane off the ground. Then, once in the air, the nozzles swing back to accelerate the Harrier to a maximum speed of around Mach .97. The nozzles help make the Harrier one of the most agile planes in the air and by swinging them forward a Harrier pilot can slow down from 966 km/h (600 mph) to a hover in just 12 seconds. Three out of four mock dogfights between Harriers and more powerful F-15 Eagles have been won by the Harriers.

Various types of Harrier are used by the armed forces of Britain, India, Spain and the United States. STOVL (Short TakeOff Vertical Landing) is the usual way to fly the Harrier as a short takeoff run allows the plane to carry a bigger load. Another load-booster for shipborne Sea Harriers is the ski jump takeoff ramp. Taking off from a ski jump pitches a Sea Harrier in an arc, like a thrown ball, which enables the plane to build up flying speed with a heavier load.

A ski jump was used on Britain's aircraft carrier *Illustrious* during the Falklands War of 1983. In this conflict, fought between Britain and Argentina in the South Atlantic, Harriers and Sea Harriers showed their outstanding manoeuvring power in battles with Argentine jets.

On May 1, 1983, 1st Lt Carlos Perona was flying a Mirage jet against British forces. He and his wingman (the number two pilot of a two-plane formation) spotted a pair of Sea Harriers flying towards them. The four jets crossed each other and turned hard, trying to get on each others' tails, into a firing position. In Perona's words, "The Sea Harrier has the ability to decelerate rapidly and when I glanced to one side I saw one of the bandits within 150 m (492 ft) of my aircraft." Seconds later the British pilot fired a missile which destroyed Perona's plane. Perona ejected safely and as he parachuted down he saw his own aircraft crash into the sea, followed a moment later by the Mirage flown by his wingman.

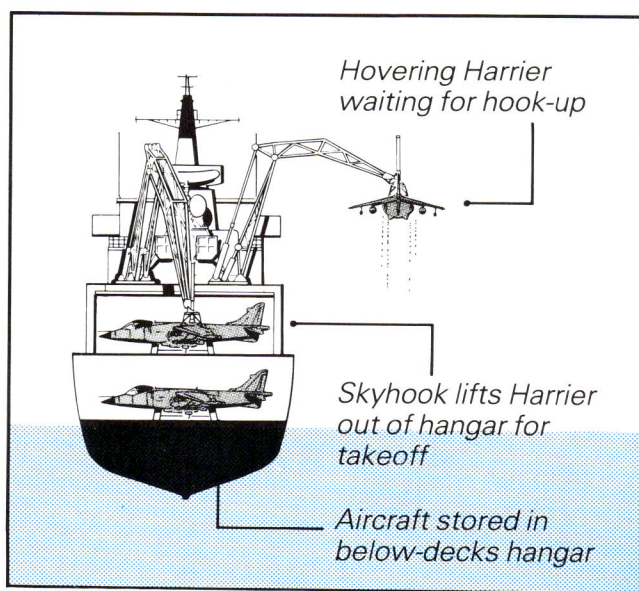

△ Future Harriers could include a supersonic machine or even this Skyhook version. Using Skyhooks, quite small ships could carry Harriers. For land use, a Skyhook could be put on the back of a large military truck.

Hovering Harrier waiting for hook-up

Skyhook lifts Harrier out of hangar for takeoff

Aircraft stored in below-decks hangar

◁ *Sea Harriers and Mirages fought many battles over the grey waters of the South Atlantic in 1983. Argentine pilots flew low to avoid radar detection, but once in close combat the delta-wing Mirage was no match for the agile STOVL fighter.*

Computers in control

To achieve a kill, a Harrier pilot has to get the enemy in his sights and fire guns or missiles. But once fired, an AIM-9L Sidewinder missile is on its own – its built-in computer steers it on a collision course to the enemy aircraft, guided by the heat of the jet exhaust. Similarly advanced computer technology is now going into aircraft as well as missiles.

The Airbus A320 is the world's first computer-controlled airliner. Unlike earlier aircraft, the A320 has no cables leading from the cockpit controls to the wings and tail. Instead of a joystick or control wheel, an A320 pilot uses a sidestick. Pressure on the sidestick is converted to digital signals by the A320's on-board computers. These send movement instructions by wire to the ailerons, flaps, elevators and rudder. The A320 also has a "glass cockpit" – the instruments are based on computer controlled TV displays, designed to be clear and easy to read.

Computer control extends throughout a flight. If an engine fails on takeoff, computers keep the jet flying in a straight line. During flight, computers adjust the controls in gusty

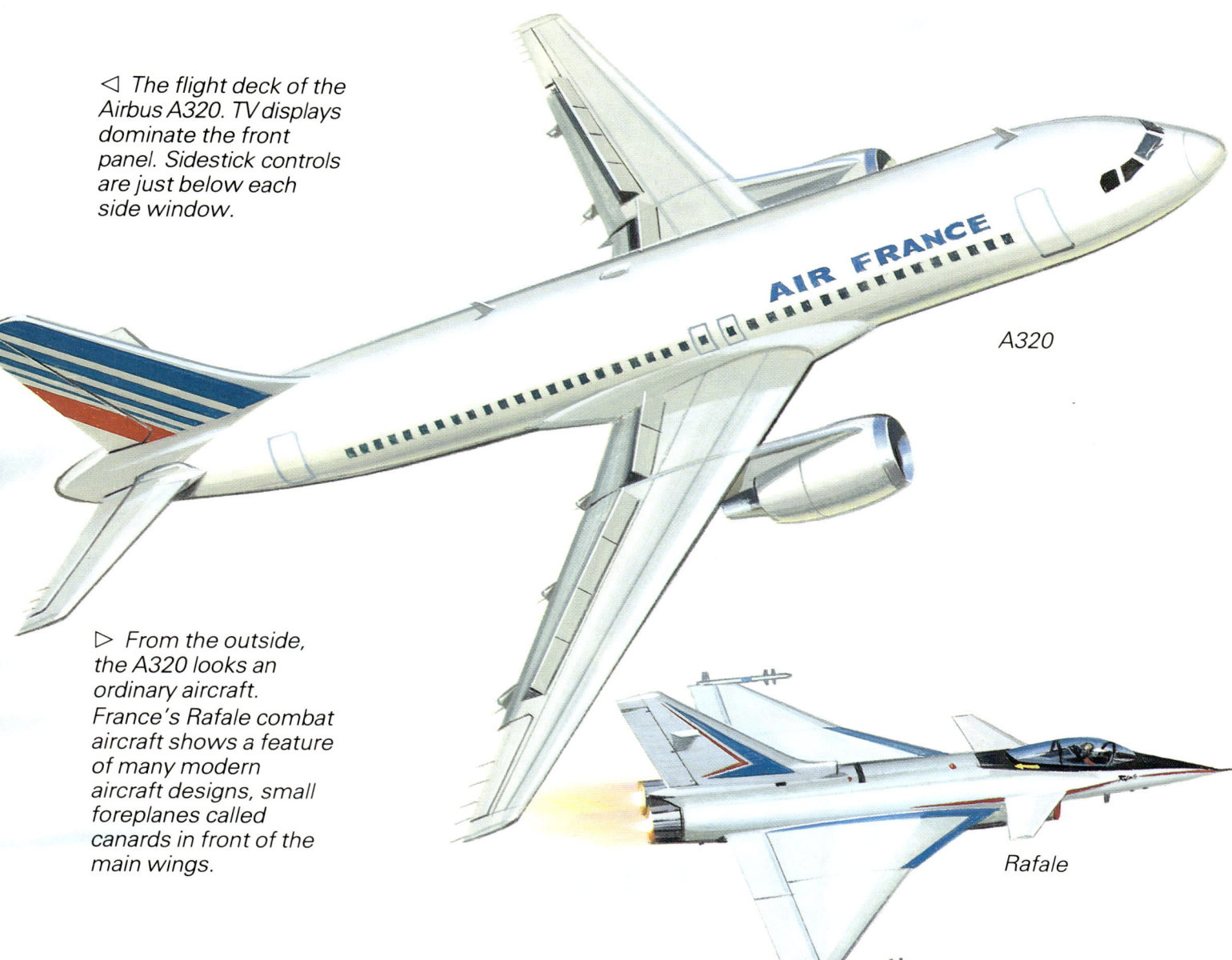

◁ *The flight deck of the Airbus A320. TV displays dominate the front panel. Sidestick controls are just below each side window.*

▷ *From the outside, the A320 looks an ordinary aircraft. France's Rafale combat aircraft shows a feature of many modern aircraft designs, small foreplanes called canards in front of the main wings.*

weather to give passengers a smooth and steady ride.

The A320's designers have included some simpler ideas to make life easy for the crew, including slide-out chart clips, recesses for coffee cups, and bins for bags and papers. And, despite all the high-tech control systems, the A320 looks and flies like a very ordinary aircraft. On long distance routes the jet cruises at a fuel efficient speed of just 786 km/h (488 mph).

Another computer control system being developed is voice control. Here, computer systems have to understand spoken command such as "SELECT GUNS" or "DISPLAY MAP". It is more difficult than it sounds, as there are other noises in the cabin, ranging from engine shriek to wind roar. A pilot's voice changes pitch, as well as ranging from a mutter to a shout. But flight tests of such systems have been made and France's new Rafale combat aircraft will have voice control built in as standard equipment. The Crouzet company working on the project says of the system, "the voice is the pilot's third hand".

Return of the propeller

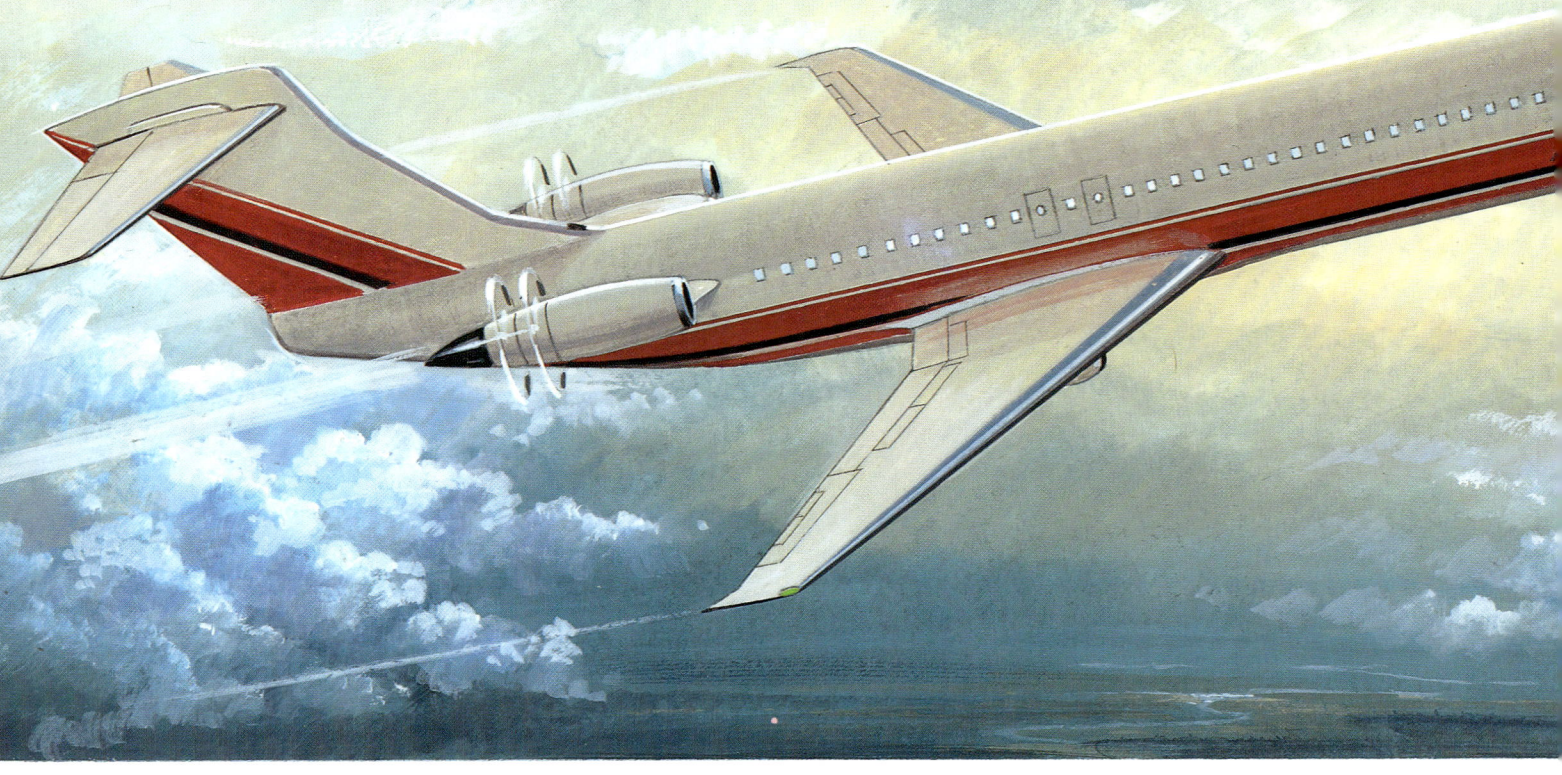

Just as computers have created a revolution in the cockpit, so engineers are changing the way aircraft are propelled. The main objectives of engine designers are reliability, economy and quietness. Propfan engines promise all three for the aircraft of the 1990s and beyond.

A propfan engine uses a jet engine "core" to turn thin, scimitar-shaped propeller blades. Curved blades can spin faster than ordinary propellers, so a propfan airliner could cruise as fast as the jetliners of today. And the propfan is highly economical, burning less than three-quarters of the fuel used by even the advanced turbofans of the A320. Pushing a large amount of air with propfan blades is more efficient than using jet thrust to push a plane along.

McDonnell Douglas plans propfan power for its rear-engined twinjet MD-80, naming the new type the MD-90 series. The propfans slot into the fuselage tail just under the fin. Engineers have come across some vibration problems but McDonnell Douglas believes its MD-90 will be the "quietest aircraft in the industry".

Aircraft makers from other countries such as France, Germany and China are also working on propfan designs. In Britain, there are plans for a highly-agile propfan battlefield fighter. By the year 2000 propellers may once again be familiar sights on new aircraft large and small.

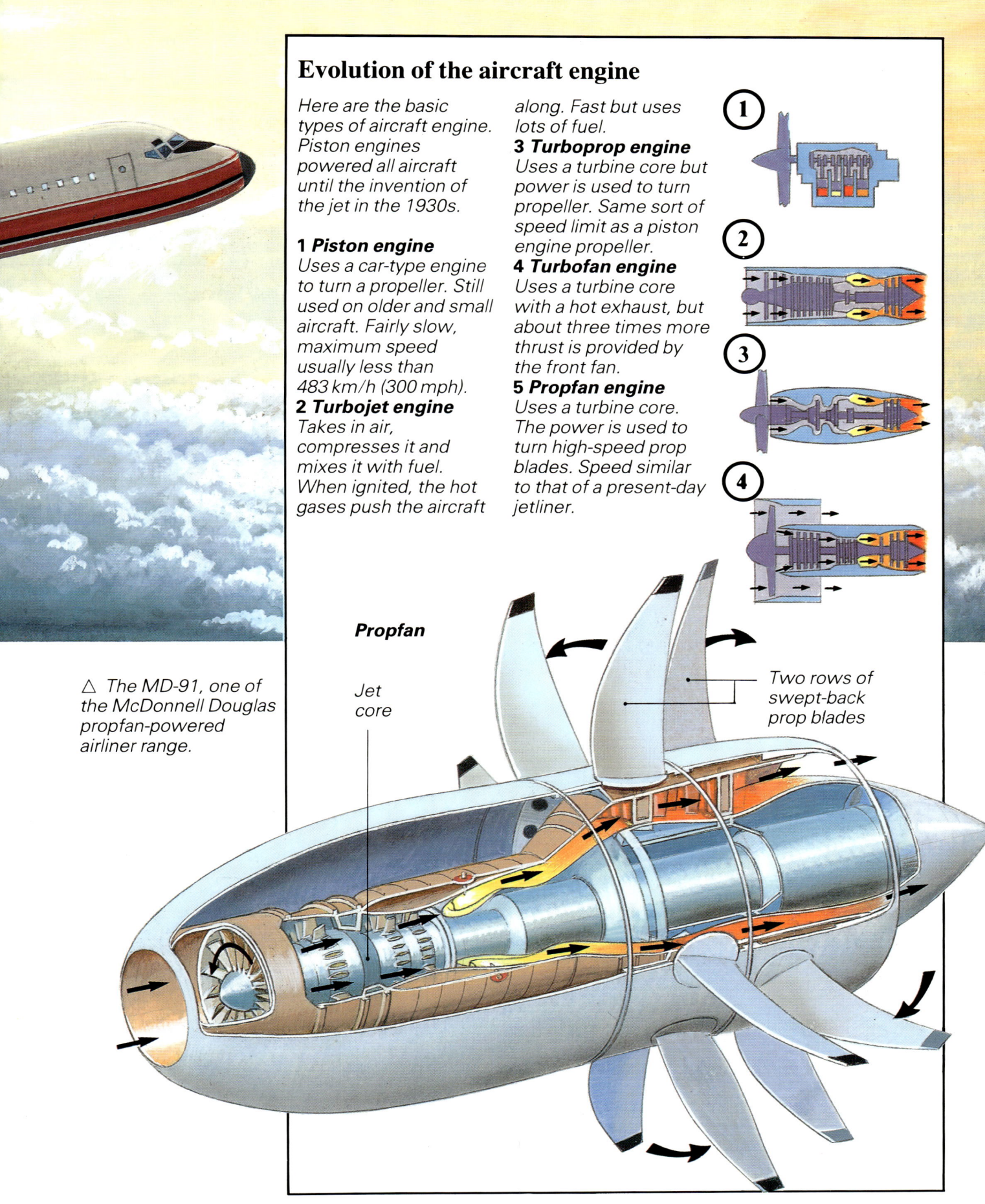

Evolution of the aircraft engine

Here are the basic types of aircraft engine. Piston engines powered all aircraft until the invention of the jet in the 1930s.

1 Piston engine
Uses a car-type engine to turn a propeller. Still used on older and small aircraft. Fairly slow, maximum speed usually less than 483 km/h (300 mph).

2 Turbojet engine
Takes in air, compresses it and mixes it with fuel. When ignited, the hot gases push the aircraft along. Fast but uses lots of fuel.

3 Turboprop engine
Uses a turbine core but power is used to turn propeller. Same sort of speed limit as a piston engine propeller.

4 Turbofan engine
Uses a turbine core with a hot exhaust, but about three times more thrust is provided by the front fan.

5 Propfan engine
Uses a turbine core. The power is used to turn high-speed prop blades. Speed similar to that of a present-day jetliner.

△ The MD-91, one of the McDonnell Douglas propfan-powered airliner range.

Propfan

Jet core

Two rows of swept-back prop blades

Weird wings

On the morning of December 14, 1984, test pilot Chuck Sewell climbed into the cockpit of a small jet, the Grumman X-29. At 9.35 am he opened up the throttle and accelerated down the lake-bed runway of Edwards Air Force Base in California. Moments later the little craft – latest in a long line of X-planes – was climbing steeply into the clear desert air. Seen from the ground, it looked as though Sewell was flying backwards – the "tailplane" was just behind the cockpit and the wings were swept forward.

In fact, the X-29 was not the first FSW (Forward Swept Wing) design. German designers produced a prototype FSW four-jet bomber during World War II and a FSW executive jet in the 1960s.

So why make a FSW X-plane in the 1980s? The answer lies partly in the increasing cost of fighter aircraft. A Battle of Britain Spitfire cost about £10,000; a modern light fighter such as the F-16, quite cheap as modern planes go, costs £10 million. FSW technology promises more agility in the air, reduced weight, and cheaper construction. Carbon fibre materials, stiffer than metal, are used for the X-29's wings. This is necessary to avoid the wingtips twisting off in violent manoeuvres. The X-29 is still flying, giving valuable information to the designers of tomorrow's fighter jets.

A new design idea is the Mission Adaptive Wing. You can see the idea of MAW if you watch a seagull flying in the wind. Look closely and you can see the gull's wings constantly flexing and adjusting to suit the moment-to-moment changes in wind forces. Though nothing like as precise or efficient as a bird's wing, the experimental MAW fitted to an F-111 fighter-bomber smooths its flight so much that the plane flies 30 per cent further on the same amount of fuel.

▷ The Grumman X-29 flies near Edwards Air Force Base with Chuck Sewell at the controls. Edwards is the new name given to Muroc Lake in 1947, the same place where, 37 years before the X-29's first flight, Chuck Yeager broke the sound barrier in the Bell X-1.

◁ General Dynamics F-111, fitted with a bird-inspired mission adaptive wing.

Fighters of tomorrow

The prototypes of the combat jets of the 1990s are already flying, testing the design features of tomorrow's air fighters.

The European Fighter Aircraft is being developed by makers from Britain, Germany, Spain and Italy. EFA has fly-by-wire controls like the Airbus A320, lighter and more reliable than rod-and-cable control systems. Unlike a plane of today, which will naturally fly a straight and level course, EFA is designed to be slightly unstable. This makes the jet more agile in the air, but no pilot has reflexes fast enough to cope with its "wobbliness", and without computers to constantly correct the plane's flightpath EFA would spin out of control and crash. Like the Grumman X-29, EFA has canard foreplanes below the cockpit. These allow quicker takeoffs, turns and other manoeuvres.

EFA pilots will also use computers to operate weapon systems. Using a computer-assisted helmet sight, a pilot simply looks at his target. The precise aiming and firing will be done by the plane's computer while the pilot concentrates on avoiding enemy fire.

Top of the secret list is the Lockheed F-19 Aurora. This is a "stealth" fighter which uses special materials and rounded shapes to make it nearly invisible to radar. Radar beams are absorbed and scattered, so a stealth plane makes barely a blip on enemy radar screens. At the moment the F-19's appearance is unknown, so the picture here is based on expert guesswork as to what such a stealth fighter could look like.

▷ A pair of new jets take to the air. At the top is an EFA European Fighter Aircraft. Below is a stealth design, possibly similar to the secret F-19 already in service.

△ EFA compared in size to a World War II Mustang fighter. The EFA is faster, heavier and more agile, but about the same size.

Airport 2000

Airports have become the busy harbours of the 20th century, centres of an intricate system of travel and commerce. A large airport includes much more than just runway, control tower and departure lounge. It is like a new kind of city, surrounded by hotels, conference centres, and cargo depots.

Future airports will have to cope with more people and more cargo. As aircraft get cheaper to operate, so more people can afford to fly. At the moment, most air cargo consists of urgent or high-value goods where the cost of transport doesn't matter too much. In the future, huge cargo planes could take much of the freight which today goes by ship. Even now, it is economic for General Motors to air-freight Italian automobile bodies to be fitted with engines in the United States.

The new planes flying in and out of Airport 2000 will include bigger versions of present-day aircraft such as the Boeing 747. Propfan airliners will fly on medium-distance routes. Miniliners and tilt-rotor transports will connect Airport 2000 with local airports. This is known as the hub-and-spoke system, where local flights feed big airports with long-distance passengers and freight.

A night view of Airport 2000. There are more night flights than at a 1980s airport. New types of aircraft are quieter than previous designs, so do not keep people awake. Magnetic-drive people-pods move passengers around the airport while computers help air traffic controllers keep the airliners moving quickly and safely.

1 Tilt-rotor lands like a helicopter, flies like an airliner.
2 Boeing 747-400 has an extended upper deck to take over 400 passengers.
3 MD-90 propfan ready for loading.
4 Business jet lines up for takeoff.
5 Giant cargolifter goes on a long trans-ocean trip. It flies near the surface, using a cushion of air under the wings to keep it aloft.
6 Control tower.
7 People-pod.
8 High-speed helicopter flies an executive to a meeting.
9 Cargo airship flies heavy goods over medium distances.
10 1980s-vintage jetliner unloading passengers. Airliners have a 20-year or longer service life, so many of today's aircraft still fly the world's air routes.

After Concorde

At present, Concorde is the only supersonic airliner. The dart-shaped aircraft carries 128 passengers and cruises at Mach 2. But Concorde is quite small, expensive to operate, noisy on takeoff and trails a supersonic boom under its flightpath, limiting it to a few overwater routes. Any future supersonic aircraft will have to carry more passengers and have a long range. If a fast aircraft has to stop to refuel, then a slower plane can catch up, defeating the point of any extra speed.

Aircraft makers are studying ideas for a 300-passenger airliner able to cruise at Mach 5. One such design is shown here, a twin-fin arrow wing machine with engines mounted under the wide fuselage section. Airliners like this won't be in service until the late 1990s, if then, but this imaginary passenger's diary shows what such a high speed trip might be like . . .

"We boarded the Los Angeles-Tokyo flight just after lunch. This flight was booked solid – there were 305 of us plus crew when the cabin door was sealed. Our aircraft is nicknamed Orient Express – it can make the Japan trip in under two hours. I was lucky to get a window seat, as the passenger cabin is very wide, with 14-abreast seating; the other people in my row had to make do with the flat-screen colour TV in the backs of the seats in front of them. The TVs are good though – you

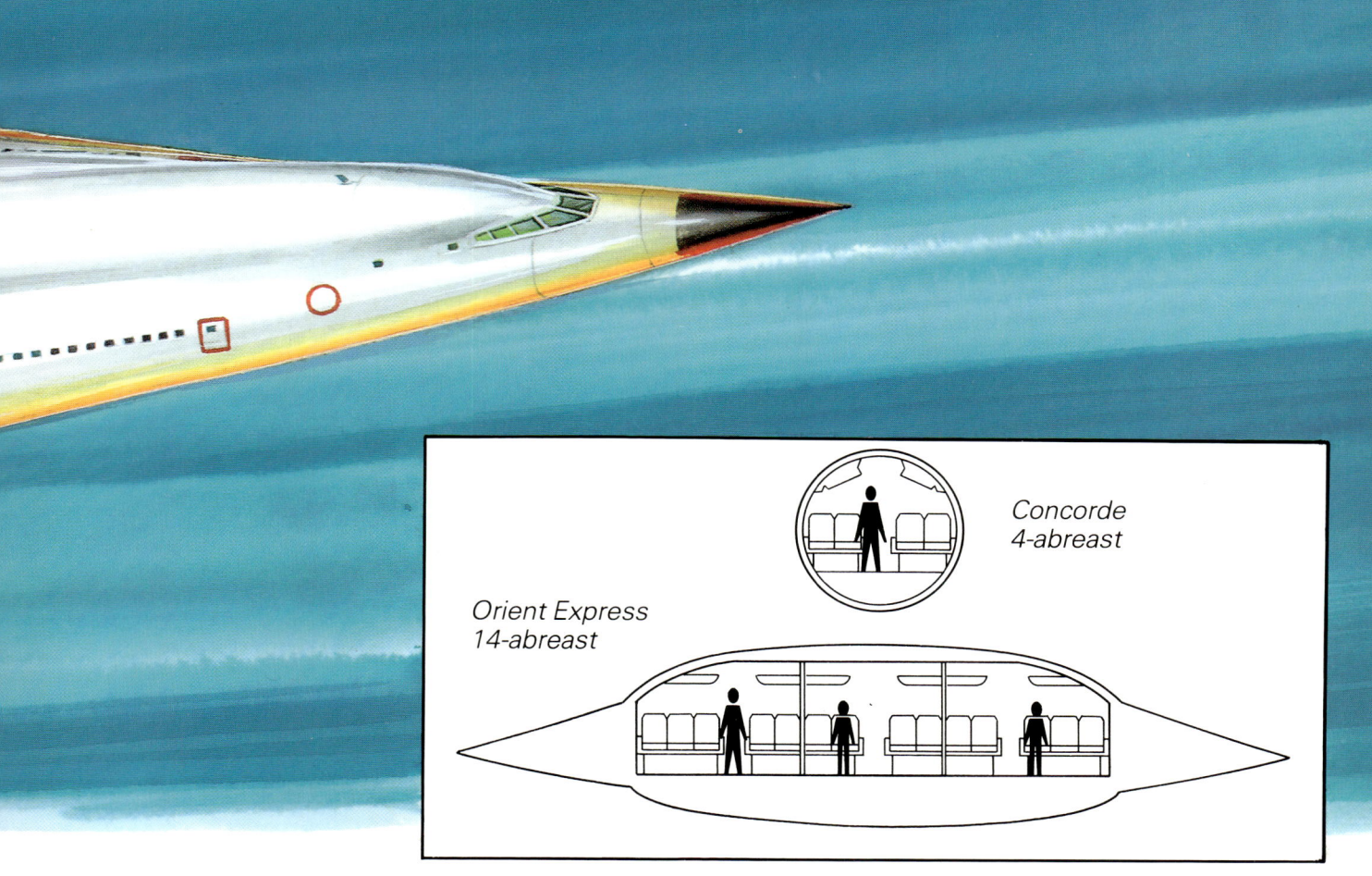

get a choice of a dozen stations as well as a view of the flight deck. You can see the captain and co-pilot sitting there. It's nice to know there are people in charge even if they only check the automatic flight equipment.

Takeoff acceleration came like an enormous hand pushing me into my seat and in moments we cleared the airport, climbing into the western sky. As the plane climbed I could see the sky changing from light blue to a deep midnight colour. We cruised at Mach 5 – over 5,000 km/h (3,000 mph). Unlike the old Concorde, Orient Express creates almost no sonic boom. We flew at 30,480 m (100,000 ft), much higher than Concorde, and the shockwave from our flight would have arrived at ground level as only a slight thud. Orient Express uses liquid methane

△ A Mach 5 airliner cruises through the thin upper air. Inside, the seats are laid out 14-abreast. Those of Concorde are just four abreast with an aisle to walk along.

fuel. Kerosene, used by subsonic aircraft, is no good for Mach 5 travel. Methane is clean-burning too, with few pollution problems. After the in-flight meal and a seat-back movie, the plane started its descent into Tokyo's Narita airport. I could see the crew monitoring their systems through my TV and over their shoulders see the runway ahead. Landing was smooth as silk – the autolander 'greased' her down as the old aviators put it. As I left the Express, I noticed something new: I had to walk through a special refrigerated walkway – the outer skin of the plane was still so hot from air friction, I'd have burned to a crisp if I had touched it".

Final frontiers

The early years of the 21st century could see the dawn of a new kind of aviation, the age of the spaceplane, a craft that flies to and from orbit with as little fuss as a normal aircraft.

There are several spaceplane designs now under development. One idea is for a mini-Shuttle carried aloft on the back of a mother plane then fired into orbit. European companies are designing the Hermes mini-Shuttle to be carried on an Ariane rocket in 1994. Similar designs are being looked at in other countries. Among the most advanced ideas is Britain's HOTOL (HOrizontal TakeOff and Landing).

This computer-controlled craft would take off an ordinary runway like an airliner, fly into space then fly back again for a normal landing. The basic idea behind all these spaceplanes is to reduce the cost of placing satellites into orbit, which at present costs about £50 million per launch. The next step would be an orbital airliner, carrying people in a low orbit around the Earth. This could cut travel time between London

and Sydney, presently a 23-hour journey, to little more than an hour.

By 2010 the first orbital transport could be making its maiden flight, but the future of aviation will not all be about travelling fast. People will still travel in ordinary aircraft for business and pleasure. And 2010 will see the 75th anniversary of the most famous airliner of all, the Douglas DC-3. In Holland, a group of keen aircraft enthusiasts, the Dutch Dakota Association, is now raising the money to put a DC-3 into storage.

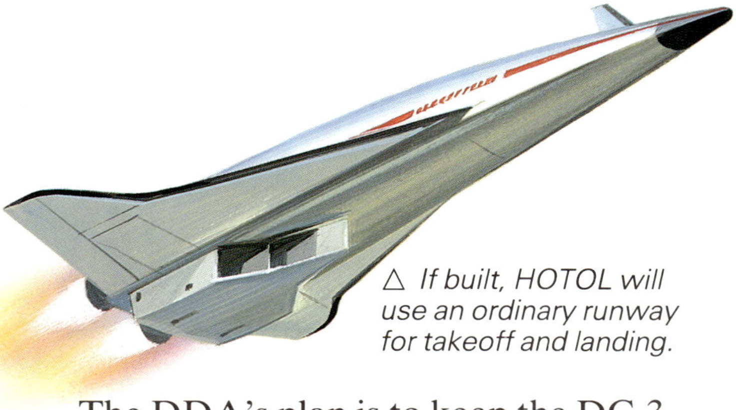

△ *If built, HOTOL will use an ordinary runway for takeoff and landing.*

The DDA's plan is to keep the DC-3 safely preserved until the 21st century. Then, the future DDA members will prepare the stored plane for an anniversary takeoff on December 17, 2010, exactly 75 years after the maiden flight of the very first DC-3.

▽ *This mini-shuttle could be carried off the ground by a 747 mother plane. Once at cruising height, the mini-shuttle would detach from the 747 and fire on-board rockets to climb away into space.*

Air data

Here are the main aircraft described in this book, shown to the same scale. The drawings of the Stealth fighter and Orient Express are based on expert estimates of their likely size and shape.

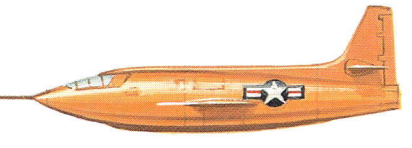

△ **Bell X-1**
Wingspan: 8.53 m (28 ft)
Length: 9.45 ft (31 ft)
Top speed: 2,736 km/h (1,700 mph)

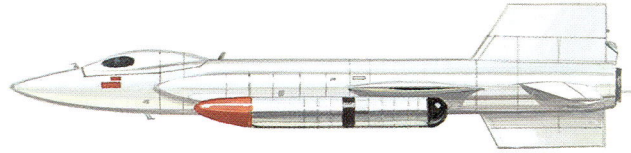

△ **North American X-15A-2**
Wingspan: 6.7 m (22 ft)
Length: 15.98 m (52 ft 5 in)
Speed: 7,274 km/h (4,520 mph)

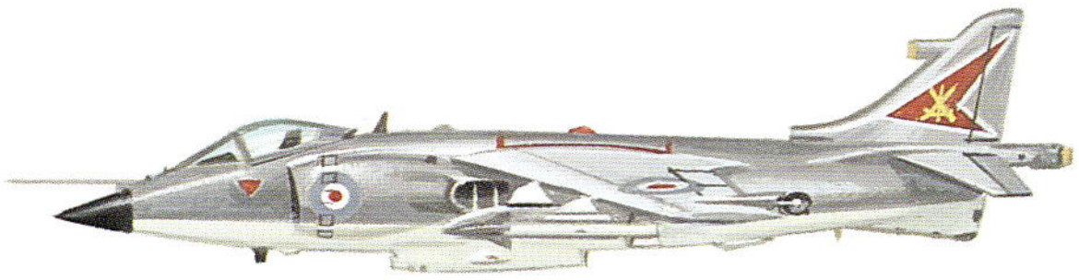

△ **British Aerospace Sea Harrier**
Wingspan: 7.7 m (25 ft 3 in)
Length: 14.5 m (47 ft 7 in)
Speed: over 1,185 km/h (736 mph)

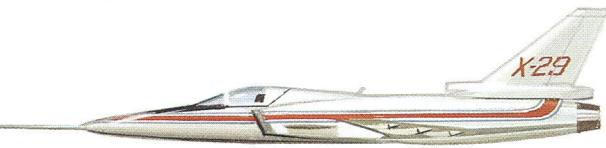

△ **Grumman X-29**
Wingspan: 8.23 m (27 ft)
Length: 14.63 m (48 ft)
Speed: 1,931 km/h (1,200 mph)

△ **Dassault Rafale A**
Wingspan: 11.2 m (36 ft 9 in)
Length: 15.8 m (51 ft 10 in)
Speed: 1,480 km/h (920 mph)

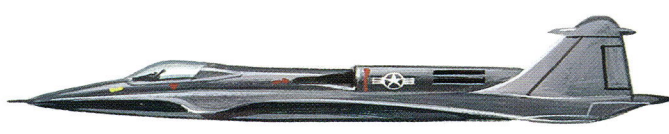

△ **Lockheed F-19 Aurora "Stealth"**
Wingspan: 9.65 m (31 ft 8 in)
Length: 18 m (59 ft)
Speed: 1,038 km/h (645 mph)

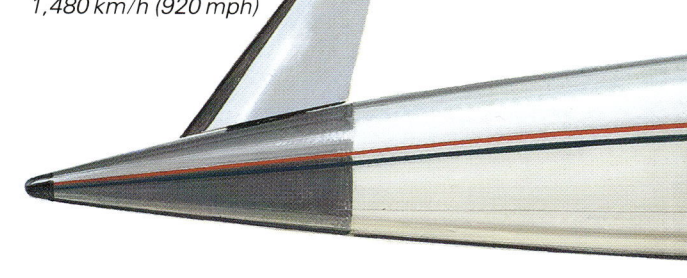

▽ **Orient Express**
Wingspan: 32 m (105 ft)
Length: 67 m (220 ft)
Speed: 5310 km/h (3,300 mph)

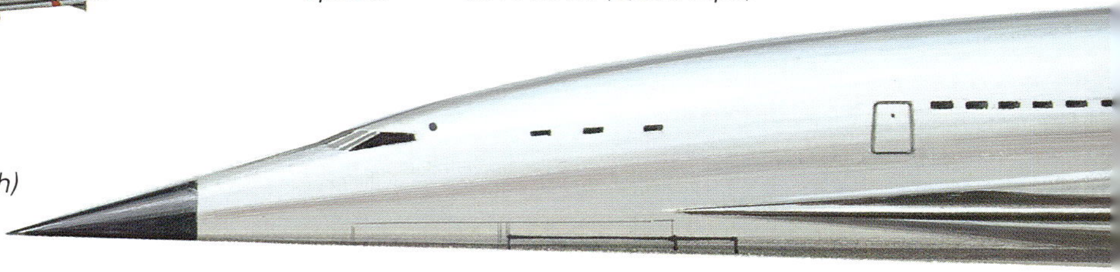

△ **Eurofighter EFA**
Wingspan: 10.5 m (34 ft 5 in)
Length: 15.75 m (51 ft 8 in)
Speed: over 1,912 km/h (1,188 mph)

△ **Airbus A320**
Wingspan: 33.91 m (111 ft 3 in)
Length: 37.57 m (123 ft 3 in)
Speed: 786 km/h (488 mph)

▽ **McDonnell Douglas MD-91**
Wingspan: 32.87 m (107 ft 10 in)
Length: 39.75 m (130 ft 5 in)
Speed: 828 km/h (515 mph)

▽ **British Aerospace/
Rolls Royce HOTOL**
Wingspan: 20.75 m (68 ft)
Length: 61 m (200 ft)
Speed: 27,800 km/h (17,270 mph) in Earth orbit

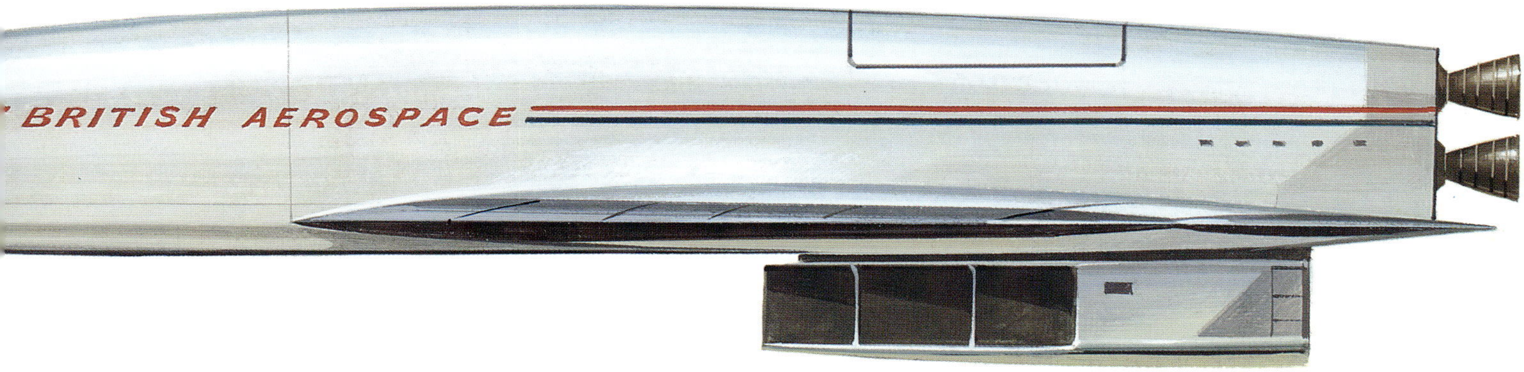

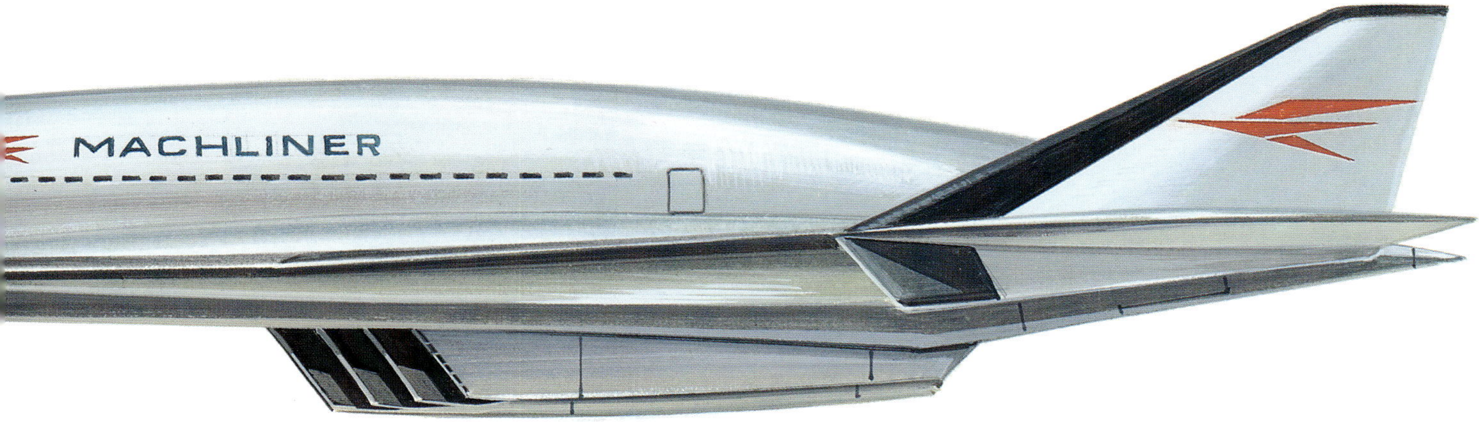

Record breakers

Ever since the earliest flights at the turn of the century, making and breaking records has been a target for aviators all over the world. Here are some records marking over 80 years of trailblazing air progress.

First speed record
Orville Wright established the first aircraft record when he made the first ever manned flight in the Wright Flyer. Speed in the air was 48 km/h (30 mph). A headwind was blowing at the time, which reduced the Flyer's speed over the ground to 10.9 km/h (6.8 mph).

Fastest biplane flight
The Italian Fiat CR 42B achieved a speed of 520 km/h (323 mph) in 1941.

Fastest piston-engined aircraft
In August 1966 Mike Carroll, of Los Angeles, California, flew his Hawker Sea Fury at 836 km/h (520 mph). The official record is held by Frank Taylor, who flew a North American Mustang at 832.12 km/h (517.055 mph) on July 30, 1983.

Fastest Atlantic airliner flight
The supersonic BAC/Aérospatiale Concorde covered the New York-London route in 2 hours 56 minutes 35 seconds on January 1, 1983.

Fastest Atlantic flight
1 hour 54 minutes, established on September 1, 1974. The aircraft was an SR-71A, flown by Major James Sullivan and Major Noel Widdifield. They flew eastbound and had to slow down halfway to be refuelled in mid-air by a KC-135 tanker aircraft. Even so, their average speed across the Atlantic was 2,908.026 km/h (1,806.963 mph).

Fastest jet aircraft
Captain Eldon Joersz and Major George Morgan Jr, flew a Lockheed SR-71A at Beale Air Base, California, on July 28, 1976. They scorched along in a straight-line flight at 3,529.56 km/h (2,193.17 mph).

Fastest aircraft
Major William Knight flew the X-15A-2 on October 3, 1967 to reach a top speed of Mach 6.7, 7,274 km/h (4,520 mph).

Highest flight
The altitude record for an aircraft taking off from a runway under its own power (rather than being air-dropped like the X-15) is held by a Soviet pilot and plane. On August 31, 1977, Aleksandr Fedotov flew his twin-turbojet MiG E-266M to a height of 37,650 m (123,524 ft).

Fastest propeller aircraft
The Soviet Tupolev Tu-114 turboprop transport has achieved 877.212 km/h (545.076 mph).

First supersonic flight
Captain Charles Yeager flew the Bell X-1 through the sound barrier on October 14, 1947. Top speed on the flight was Mach 1.015, 1,078 km/h (670 mph)

First flight around the world, unrefuelled
Dick Rutan and Jeanna Yeager took off in their Voyager aircraft on December 14, 1986, flying westbound from Edwards Air Force Base, California. They landed nine days later on December 23. The flight covered 40,252 km (25,012 miles).

Speed into orbit
The Space Shuttle Columbia hit 26,715 km/h (16,600 mph) on its way into orbit on April 12, 1981.

▽ The world's fastest jet, the two-seat Lockheed SR-71A

Glossary

Ablative coating
Special material designed to gradually burn away with friction heat, leaving the aircraft structure underneath unharmed by the high temperature.

Air friction
Heat caused by air molecules rubbing against an airframe at high speed. You can cause much the same effect by rubbing your hands together very quickly.

Canard foreplane
Small lifting surface mounted in front of the main wing. Can be used in place of or in addition to tail surfaces. Designed to increase the agility of an aircraft.

Dogfight
Name for fighter planes manoeuvring in kill-or-be-killed air combat.

Dump valve
Valve built into fuel system of many aircraft. Designed to dump or vent off fuel into the air in emergency situations.

Hub-and-spoke
Type of airline operation in which small airliners fly passengers from outlying districts along "spoke" routes to a big "hub" airport. Here the passengers change from the small planes to big long-range aircraft which fly to international destinations.

Jumbo jet
Nickname often used for the biggest jetliner in service, the Boeing 747.

Liquid methane
Condensed form of methane gas. When supercooled in a specially sealed container, the gas turns to liquid in much the same way as steam turns to water when cooled. When released through a valve the methane expands to form a gas again before being burned.

Mach 1
The speed of sound, about 1,225 km/h (762 mph) at sea level, slowing with height to about 1,062 km/h (660 mph) at 12 km (7.45 miles). Above this height the speed of sound stays constant. Mach 2 is twice the speed of sound and so on. The Mach system is named after Ernst Mach, an Austrian scientist.

Orbit
Curving path an object such as the Space Shuttle takes as it goes around the Earth.

Propfan
New type of engine using a jet engine core to drive thin-bladed curved propellers. Each of the MD-90 airliner's propfan engines has two sets of propfan blades rotating in opposite directions.

Prototype
The first of a new kind of aircraft, used for much test flying. Any modifications are built into production machines.

Ramjet
Type of tube-shaped jet engine. At high speeds air flows in the front, is compressed in a narrow central "throat", mixes with fuel and is burned. The hot gases rush out of the back, pushing the ramjet at high speed.

Ski jump
Type of takeoff ramp with a curved-up lip, used on new types of small aircraft carriers.

Skyhook
System designed to hook up Harrier jets in mid-air for storage on board ship. Using Skyhook, a ship needs no large, flat runway area for its on-board aircraft.

Stealth
Name given to aircraft made with special materials and curved shapes to absorb and scatter radar beams. The effect is near-invisibility to enemy radar so such an aircraft can fly undetected, in a "stealthy" way.

Stratosphere
Name for the part of the atmosphere stretching from about 9 km (6 miles) to 24 km (15 miles) above the Earth. Most clouds and weather occur below this, in the troposphere.

Supersonic boom
As an aircraft passes the speed of sound, the air forced to either side is compressed briefly to form a shock wave. The shock wave expands into the atmosphere, like the ripples in a pool when you throw a pebble into the water. As the shockwave hits ground level, we hear it as a double-thud booming sound.

Swing-wing
Type of aircraft which has wings which stick out straight for takeoff and landing. For high-speed flight the wings move back into a swept position, like a dart. Swing-wing aircraft include such types as the General Dynamics F-111, Panavia Tornado and Grumman F-14 Tomcat.

Tilt-rotor
Type of aircraft which uses large rotors for vertical takeoff and landing. The rotors point up for takeoff and landing then tilt to the front for forward flight.

Index

AIM-9L Sidewinder 14
Airbus A320 14, 15, 16, 20, 28
Argentina 12
Ariane 26
Armstrong, Neil 9
Atlantic 30

B-29 Superfortress 6, 7
B-52 Stratofortress 8
BAC/Aérospatiale Concorde 15, 24, 25, 30
Battle of Britain 18
Beale Air Base 30
Bell X-1 6, 7, 18, 28, 30
Bell X-1A 7
Boeing 707 10
Boeing 747 4, 10, 11, 22, 23, 27, 31
Britain 6, 12, 20
British Aerospace Harrier, Sea Harrier 12, 13, 14, 28, 31
British Aerospace/Rolls Royce HOTOL 26, 27, 29

California 6, 18, 30
Cardenas, Bob 7
Carroll, Mike 30
China 16
Columbia 30
Concorde (see BAC)
Crouzet company 15

Dassault Rafale 15, 28
De Havilland Comet 10
Douglas DC-3 10, 27
Dutch Dakota Association 27

Edwards Air Force Base 18, 30
Eurofighter EFA 20, 29

F-15 Eagle 12
F-16 18
F-111 (see General Dynamics)
Falklands War 12
Fedotov, Aleksandr 30

Fiat CR 42B 30
France 15, 16
FSW 18

General Dynamics F-111 18, 31
General Motors 22
Germany 6, 16, 20
Glamorous Glennis 6
Grumman F-14 Tomcat 31
Grumman X-29 18, 20, 29

Harrier, Sea Harrier (see British Aerospace)
Hawker Sea Fury 30
Hermes 26
Holland 27
HOTOL (see British Aerospace)
Hydro 2000 10, 11

India 12
Italy 20

Japan 24
Joersz, Captain Eldon 30
jumbo jet 10, 11, 31

KC-135 tanker 30
Knight, Major William 5, 8, 30

Lockheed F-19 Aurora 20, 29

Lockheed Hercules 10, 11
Lockheed SR-71, SR-71A 4, 30
London 26, 30
Los Angeles 24, 30

Mach, Ernst 31
MAW 18
McDonnell Douglas MD-80 16
McDonnell Douglas MD-90 16, 23, 31
McDonnell Douglas MD-91 17, 29
MiG E-266M 30
Mirage jet 12, 13
Moon 9
Morgan Jr, Major George 30
Muroc Lake 6, 18
Mustang (see North American)

Narita airport 25
New York 30
North American Mustang 20, 30
North American X-15, X-15A-2 5, 8, 9, 28, 30

Orient Express 24, 25, 29

Panavia Tornado 31
Perona, 1st Lt Carlos 12
piston engine 17

propfan 16, 17, 22, 31

Rafale (see Dassault)
Rutan, Dick 30

Sewell, Chuck 18
ski jump 12, 31
Skyhook 12, 31
sound barrier 6, 7, 30
South Atlantic 12
Space Shuttle, Shuttle Orbiter 5, 8, 30, 31
Spain 12, 20
Spitfire 18
stealth aircraft 20, 28, 31
STOVL 12, 13
Sullivan, Major James 30
Sydney 27

Taylor, Frank 30
Tokyo 24
Tupolev Tu-114 30
turbofan engine 17
turbojet engine 17
turboprop engine 17, 30

United States 6, 12, 22

voice control 15
Voyager 30

Widdifield, Major Noel 30
World War II 6, 18, 20
Wright brothers 4
Wright Flyer 4, 30
Wright, Orville 4, 30

X-5 8
X-14 8
X-15, X-15A-2 (see North American)
XLR99-RM-2 rocket engine 5

Yeager, Captain Charles "Chuck" 6, 7, 18, 30
Yeager, Jeanna 30